HISTORY UNSCHOOLED INVENTIONS FROM THE STONE AGE

BY JJ CARROLL

HISTORY UNSCHOOLED
INVENTIONS FROM THE STONE AGE

First Published in the United States by Quality Business Communications, Inc., Reading, Pennsylvania, USA. 2023

Copyright © 2023 by JJ Carroll. All rights reserved.
Illustrations by Gholamreza Shoghmand Nazarloo
Design by Abdul Moiz(fiverr: abdul_moiez)

Manufactured in the United States of America
First Printing

ISBN: 978-1-7328147-3-8

HistoricBooksforKids.com is a subsidiary of Quality Business Communications Inc. This book also contains activities, videos and citations that link to other organizations and brands. Neither the publisher nor author is affiliated in any way with these other organizations or brands. We do not receive payment from them and are not endorsed by them. Over time, some links may become broken or organizations may cease to exist.

No part of this publication may be reproduced, stored or transmitted in any form or by any means, electronic, mechanical, photocopying, recording, scanning, or otherwise without written consent permission from the publisher. It is illegal to copy this book, post it to a website, or distribute it by any other means without permission. Write to info@qubcomm.com.

First edition.

ACKNOWLEDGEMENTS

My greatest thanks goes to Diane Strauss, a former homeschooler and fellow lover of history, and my sister, who was so helpful in researching books, sharing ideas and cheerleading the process through hours and hours of cross country phone calls each and every Saturday morning — and often during the week — over the many months it took to write this.

TABLE OF CONTENTS

How To Use This Book 1
Tips To Access The Novels And Other Books For Free 3
How To Research Historic Topics 4
Try Out Your New Research Skills 7

Stone Age - Prehistory to 4000 BCE 8
   Suggested Books, Movies And More 9

The Hand Axe - 1.4 Million BCE 13
   Reading, Writing, Research 14
   Steam Activities And More 15
   Invention Discussion Page 19

Fire - 1 Million BCE 20
   Reading, Writing, Research 21
   Steam Activities And More 22
   Invention Discussion Page 26

Clothing - 500,000 to 100,000 BCE 27
   Reading, Writing, Research 29
   Steam Activities And More 30
   Invention Discussion Page 35

Written Communication - 70,000 BCE 36
   Reading, Writing, Research 38
   Steam Activities And More 39
   Invention Discussion Page 43

Medicine And First Aid - 60,000 to 31 000 BCE 44
   Reading, Writing, Research 45
   Steam Activities And More 46
   Invention Discussion Page 51

Pottery And Baskets - 4,000 to 16,000 BCE 52
   Reading, Writing, Research 53
   Steam Activities And More 54
   Invention Discussion Page 59

Agriculture - 8,500 BCE **60**
Reading, Writing, Research 61
Steam Activities And More 63
Invention Discussion Page 68

Wheel - 4,500 BCE **69**
Reading, Writing, Research 70
Steam Activities And More 71
Invention Discussion Page 75

Puzzle Solutions **76**

HOW TO USE THIS BOOK

Students will learn history through human inventions

It has long been true that necessity is the mother of invention. Since the dawn of our species, we've been thinking and creating based on our needs and lifestyles. This book will help students learn about the Stone Age by studying the most important discoveries of the times.

The UN-textbook helps students think on their own

The concept is to allow students to think and learn without a textbook full of facts to memorize (and quickly forget after the quiz). Instead, kids can immerse themselves in stories to get in the mindset.

Then, they'll find thought provoking questions and topics to research, write about and discuss. How they do that is up to you... or them. Should they write an essay? Take sides in a formal debate? Or simply discuss over dinner?

Encourage reading, writing and research along the way

This book encourages all types of reading and writing as well as oral presentations. Besides the lists of fiction and nonfiction books, each chapter has opportunities for writing, critical thinking, research and discussion.

Research is an important life skill for anyone to have regardless of whether a student is college bound. Learn more about research skills on page 4. You may wish to start there before you begin the historic units, especially with older students. They'll have ample opportunity to use their newfound research skills throughout the year.

Have fun with STEAM-based activities

Since each topic is an invention, it was easy to incorporate Science, Technology, Engineering, Art, and Math into the learning.

Look for these icons in the Activities section of each chapter.

Science   Technology   Engineering   Art   Mathematics

The whole family can learn together

If you have multiple students in various grades, they all can learn together. Each invention chapter includes family-friendly activities at all education levels:

- ➤ **Level 1** indicates easy activities for elementary students.
- ➤ **Level 2** involves more reading and simple research skills for middle school ages.
- ➤ **Level 3** encourages a higher level of research and writing skills for high school age students.

You or your older students can choose to do all of the activities, or just those on the higher levels.

How historic novels help kids learn about different times

Fiction is a great way to get kids interested in a topic. Especially when the alternative is a textbook. These fictional stories are for kids to experience the past. The education part should be subtle. The side effect? Kids who read!

We include a list of recommended fiction (and movies) that take place during, or focus on a certain aspect of, the Stone Age. Feel free to add to the list if you know of books that we missed or as new books are published. Ask your librarian or local bookstore owner for suggestions.

You can allow students to absorb the history on their own. Or you can have your own family book club and discuss the stories as well. Talk about the inventions learned, or challenge them to research and discuss any suspected fallacies in the stories. Fiction means it's not all fact. Students can have fun busting myths and catching where the author took creative license.

Print out answer sheets, coloring pages and more

Be sure to download and print our FREE History Unschooled Stone Age Print Pack to get hotlinks to the resources, plus printable worksheets and all the activity pages in this book to help you sort and store written materials for your homeschool record keeping.

Scan this QR code to get the History Unschooled: Inventions from the Stone Age print pack

TIPS TO ACCESS THE NOVELS AND OTHER BOOKS FOR FREE

Look for the suggested movies and books at your local library. If not available, your librarian may be able to request it in from a sister library.

If your child has a smart device and can download apps, consider a membership with Libby, which works through the library system to lend eBooks for free.

You might also check used book stores in your area or online, such as Thriftbooks.com, to get books at a discounted price.

Historic Books for Kids is a proud supporter of *your* local bookstore.

If FREE or discount isn't available, you can buy online AND support local at the same time. Historic Books for Kids bookshop uses **Bookshop.org** (https://bookshop.org/info/about-us), which is a nonprofit organization that supports local brick and mortar book stores instead of mega online retailers.

Most of the books listed on pages 9 and 10 are available at:
https://bookshop.org/shop/HistoricBooksforKids.

HOW TO RESEARCH HISTORIC TOPICS

Research is a process not an action

The goal of research is to fully understand the source data and satisfactorily answer questions as accurately as possible.

Typically the process goes like this:

1. Ask your question
2. Choose your sources and gather data
3. Sort and process the information
4. Develop your answer
5. Cite your sources

Ask your question

What is it you want to know? This is where you plan your investigation. Be prepared to change or form new questions as you uncover facts.

For example, you want to know who invented the wheel. As you perform your research, you realize that the wheel existed before recorded history. That means you probably won't ever be able to answer "who" specifically invented it. The answer doesn't exist.

But you might be able to determine approximately when it was invented based on archaeological evidence. You may also learn the oldest evidence of use to conclude where it was likely invented. This can help narrow down your search to a specific species, people or tribe.

Choose your sources and gather data

There are three kinds of sources:

1. Primary
2. Secondary
3. Tertiary

1. Primary Source:

Direct evidence about your topic. This includes things like archaeological evidence, account books (such as the *Domesday Book*), boat passenger lists, diaries and other contemporary writings. "Contemporary" means it was written or recorded by someone who personally witnessed the event, experienced the time, or created the data.

The reference section of a library may lead you to Primary sources. You can also consult:

- Library of Congress at https://www.loc.gov/programs/teachers/getting-started-with-primary-sources/finding/
- National Archives at https://www.archives.gov/education/research/primary-sources
- Smithsonian at https://learninglab.si.edu/collections/primary-sources/MhkNadPOAl59VFw1

2. Secondary Source:

A commentary or interpretation of a primary source, such as a journal article or news story. This type of source includes retellings from someone who was not present during the event, even if the person was alive at the time.

3. Tertiary Source:

This third level source can refer to someone else's assembly of information based on consolidated primary and secondary sources. Wikipedia, academic papers, magazine articles, and blog posts fall into this category.

Tertiary sources can help guide students to primary and secondary sources through their citations. Parents and teachers might encourage Level 2 students to use and cite trusted tertiary sources while encouraging Level 3 students to consult the primary sources for themselves to make their own interpretation.

Sort and process the information

Four blind men found an animal. One touched a leg and was sure he found a goat. One found the tail and thought it was a giraffe. One felt the fur and believed it was a dog. The last had the belly and thought it was a horse. None of them had the whole picture; therefore they couldn't agree on the type of animal they had found. The hungry lion ate them all.

No single source should lead you to a final conclusion because no single source will have all the data. There's an old saying that history was written by the victors. That means the stories you hear about antiquity - even when told by a primary source - can be incomplete, one-sided or wrong, especially if the author had an agenda or prejudice.

An agenda refers to why something was written. What purpose did it serve? Who did the writing and for whom did they write?

A prejudice can refer to the author's leanings and if they wanted someone in the story to look bad - or good.

Agendas and prejudices can impact how the story was told, including omissions, exaggerations, and outright fiction. Secondary sources are based on interpretations and often hearsay, which can likewise be wrong. Sometimes the wrong story can be passed down for generations.

Consider the story of young George Washington chopping down a cherry tree and telling the truth about it to his father. For nearly two centuries, Americans believed it as hardcore fact. It wasn't until a researcher noticed there was no primary source for the story. In fact, the first time it was written was after Washington's death. The public was hungry for information about their hero and a minister and bookseller named Mason Locke Weems delivered. He first published Washington's biography in 1800. Then he updated it several times and the cherry tree story was added in the 5th edition in 1806. Washington did have a reputation for honesty and maybe Weems wanted to encourage honesty for kids. Or maybe he was just looking to sell books with legendary stories. The point is, the cherry tree event probably never happened.

Likewise, there's no actual evidence that famous characters like Robin Hood and King Arthur ever existed. But the stories have some root possibilities for which the primary sources may be lost to antiquity or haven't been found yet.

The key to successful historic research is to consult as many sources as possible. See if primary sources exist and, if so, what different sources have to say. See how their stories differ and how they are the same. Consider any potential prejudices and agendas. Keep in mind what the primary source, data, archaeological dig or other information does NOT tell you.

Then see how different secondary sources interpret the event. Review tertiary sources and decide if you agree with them. If you don't agree, look for evidence to support your disagreement.

Develop your answer

After all that research and myth busting, you can finally draw a conclusion based on the evidence collected. Do you have any questions that remain unanswered due to lack of evidence? Is there enough evidence to support a possibility, even if not certainty? Write your conclusion so it reflects facts only and not your own or someone else's opinion.

Cite your sources

A proper citation gives full credit to the originator of the data and includes enough information to enable a reader to find the source for themselves. Citing your source also gives you the opportunity to reflect on the reliability of the source information.

There are several ways to cite a source. Some methods are for academic use and others are for business. They may also vary by field. Historians usually use citations as presented in *Chicago Manual of Style*. You can find and learn more at
https://www.chicagomanualofstyle.org/tools_citationguide.html.

TRY OUT YOUR NEW RESEARCH SKILLS

Legends: Fiction vs. Fact is 32 pages of fun stories that show the importance of research skills. It includes games and a legendary research project kids can try on their own.

Get it on the Historic Books for Kids website (www.historicbooksforkids).

STONE AGE

PREHISTORY TO 4000 BCE

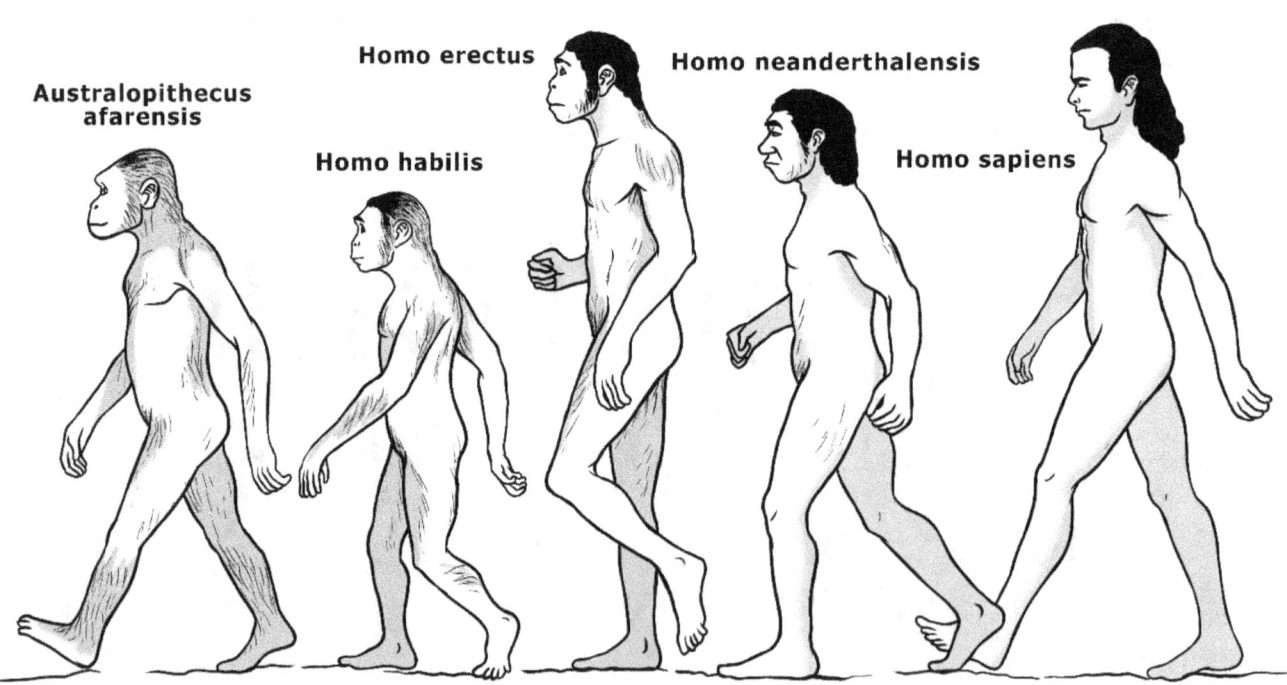

SUGGESTED BOOKS, MOVIES AND MORE

Books and movies can help kids become enthusiastic about the Stone Age. Here is a list of suggested books and more. Encourage them also to suggest their own. Ask your local librarian for new and popular books that take place during the Stone Age or that feature the inventions used in ancient times or settings. See page 3 for no-cost and low-cost ways to get these books.

Stories and Novels

- The First Dog by Jan Brett (Preschool to 7 years)
- UG: Boy Genius of the Stone Age and his Search for Soft Trousers by Raymond Briggs (Preschool to 7 years)
- Stone Age Boy by Satoshi Kitamura (4-7 years)
- The First Drawing by Mordicai Gerstein (4-8 years)
- Sunset of the Sabertooth by Mary Pope Osborne (5-8 years)
- Lucy and Andy Neanderthal by Jeffrey Brown (7-10 years)
- Stone Age Tales: The Great Cave by Terry Deary (7-9 years)
- The Wild Way Home by Sophie Kirtley (7-12 years)
- The Stone Age: Hunters, Gatherers and Woolly Mammoths by Marcia Williams (7-12 years)
- Stig of the Dump by Clive King (8-11 years)
- The Wolf's Boy by Susan Williams Beckhorn (8-12 years)
- Hubert Invents The Wheel by Monte and Claire Montgomery. (9-12 years)
- The Stolen Spear by Saviour Pirotta (Teens and Young Adult)
- Touching Spirit Bear by Ben Mikaelsen (12 years and up: Not a Stone Age tale, but one of brutal survival and symbolism)
- Wolf Brother by Michelle Paver (12-17 years)
- The Clan of the Cave Bear: Earth's Children, Book One by Jean M. Auel. A clan of Neanderthals find and raise an injured Cro-Magnon girl whose intelligence gets her into trouble as she matures into womanhood. (Age 17 and up. Warning: includes acts of violence, including sexual violence.)
- Mutant Message Down Under by Marlo Morgan (Young adult/adult: Not a Stone Age tale. An American woman goes on an Australian walkabout with an aborigine tribe.)

Nonfiction Books

- Life In The Stone Age: L2 DK Reader by Deborah Lock (5-7 years)
- Prehistoric People by Donald Grant (5-7 years)
- Hands-on History: Stone Age by Charlotte Hurdman (5-8 years)
- My Best Book of Early People by Margaret Hynes (5-8 years)
- DK Find Out! Stone Age by DK (6-9 years)
- Mega Meltdown: The Weird and Wonderful Animals of the Ice Age by Jack Tite (7-10 years)
- Hit It! History of Tools by Dona Herweck Rice (7-11 years)
- When We Became Humans: Our Incredible Evolutionary Journey by Michael Bright (7 - 11 years)
- The History Detective Investigates: Stone Age to Iron Age by Clare Hibbert
- Ox, House, Stick: The History of Our Alphabet by Don Robb (8-12 years)
- Stone Age People (Make It Work! History) by Andrew Haslam (10 years and up)

Movies (fiction)

- Ice Age (2002) Starring the voices of Denis Leary, John Leguizamo, Ray Romano; Written by Michael J. Wilson, Michael Berg, Peter Ackerman; Directed by Chris Wedge, Carlos Saldanha. Animated story about a woolly mammoth, saber-toothed tiger, and a sloth, who find a man child and try to return it to its village. Rated PG for mild peril.
- Early Man (2018) Starring the voices of Eddie Redmayne, Tom Hiddleston, Maisie Williams, and Timothy Spall; Written by Mark Burton and James Higginson; Directed by Nick Park. Stone Age meets the Bronze Age on the football field ("soccer" field in America) in this animated comedy. Rated PG for rude humor and some action.
- The Flintstones" (1994) Starring John Goodman, Rick Moranis and Rosie O'Donnell; Written by Tom S. Parker, Jim Jennewein and Steven E. de Souza; Directed by Brian Levant. Kids can have fun busting all the inaccuracies in this tale about the Flintstones and the Rubbles, 1960's television show's "modern stone-age families". Rated PG for some mild innuendos.
- The Croods (2013) Starring the voices of Emma Stone, Ryan Reynolds, and Nicolas Cage; Written by Chris Sanders, Kirk DeMicco, and John Cleese; Directed by Kirk DeMicco and Chris Sanders. The Croods are n eccentric family of cavemen, who are forced into the wilderness of the unknown to find a new home. Rated PG for some scary action.

- Alpha (2018) Starring Kodi Smit-McPhee, Jóhannes Haukur Jóhannesson, and Marcin Kowalczyk; Written by Daniele Sebastian Wiedenhaupt and Albert Hughes; Directed by Albert Hughes. A young prehistoric man has an accident and is presumed dead by his hunting party. He must use his skills to survive and find his way home. Rated PG-13 for some intense peril.

- Cast Away (2000). Starring Tom Hanks and Helen Hunt; Written by William Broyles Jr.; Directed by Robert Zemeckis. A FedEx executive undergoes a physical and emotional transformation after crash landing on a deserted island. He has to learn how to survive on his own and ultimately how to escape the isolation. He teaches himself fire building, rope making and other basic but necessary skills. Rated PG-13 for intense action sequences and some disturbing images.

Documentaries, videos, virtual tours and more (nonfiction).

- Prehistoric Art and Artifacts - Virtual Tour Available at: Joy of Museums Virtual Tours. https://joyofmuseums.com/prehistoric-art-and-artifacts-virtual-tour/. The earliest human artifacts showing evidence of sustainable workmanship with an artistic purpose existed by 40,000 years ago.

- The Dordogne, France: Lascaux's Prehistoric Cave Paintings. Rick Steve's Europe. Available at: https://youtu.be/UnSq0c7jM-A. From about 18,000 to 10,000 BCE, prehistoric people painted deep inside caves in what is today the Dordogne region of France.

- Tools & Food | The Smithsonian Institution's Human Origins Program (si.edu) at https://humanorigins.si.edu/human-characteristics/tools-food. Includes educational videos on a variety of Stone Age topics.

- Göbekli Tepe: UNESCO World Heritage Site. Visit https://whc.unesco.org/en/list/1572 to learn about the world's oldest known monumental structure, built by Neolithic people before the invention of pottery.

- Human Lineage: From Encyclopedia Britannica, available at https://www.britannica.com/science/human-evolution#/media/1/275670/73009. Learn about the evolution of early humans and who may have been responsible for some of the first inventions

- Mesopotamian Monuments Virtual Field Trip for Grades 6-8. This 50-minute tour is available at: https://hmane.harvard.edu/virtual-field-trips. Reservations required and there may be a fee for this virtual field trip.

- Archaeological Institutes of America Archaeological Digs. Interactive Digs are an opportunity to see an excavation unfold in real time. Archaeologists post regular updates from the field, answer questions, and describe life on a dig. Visit InteractiveDigs.com to find a list of dig sites.

- ➢ Ancient Mesopotamia 101 video. Available at: https://education.nationalgeographic.org/resource/ancient-mesopotamia-101/. Learn how this "land between two rivers" became the birthplace of the world's first cities, advancements in math and science, and the earliest evidence of literacy and a legal system.
- ➢ Watch the building of a potter's wheel, Stone Age style: https://youtu.be/Gqhxe_pL6Ws.

THE HAND AXE

1.4 Million BCE

Homo erectus would have used the objects around them as tools. For example, a stick or branch might have been a weapon or may have helped them knock food out of a tree. Stones were easy to grab, abundant to find and could be used to hammer things, pound or grind food, or throw to scare away predators.

Oldewan is the name given to a style of tool that dates as far back as 2.9 million years ago by ancient Hominins in Africa. These early humans simply shaped a rock to suit their purpose, such as make it more comfortable to hold so they can use it to pound other things.

The Acheulean hand axe is the earliest known man-made tool. There's no evidence to show who first made it or what they did with this new tool. It's possible someone simply found a rock with a sharp edge and saw that it cut stuff. Or perhaps someone was shaping a pounding rock and accidentally chipped it to the point of sharpness.

Once they had a sharp edge, they may have tested its uses like sharpening the end of a stick or cutting meat. At some point someone perfected the shape of the hand axe with a fat, rounded end for holding and a hard business end for cutting. Imagine their reaction when sparks flew from the flint stone!

The hand axe was in use from about 1.76 million years ago until about 200,000 years ago. These ancient artifacts have been found all over Europe, Africa and Asia.

Source:

Corbey R, Jagich A, Vaesen K, Collard M. The Acheulean handaxe: More like a bird's song than a beatles' tune? Evol Anthropol. 2016 Jan-Feb;25(1):6-19. doi: 10.1002/evan.21467. PMID: 26800014; PMCID: PMC5066817. Available at: https://www.ncbi.nlm.nih.gov/pmc/articles/PMC5066817/.

READING, WRITING, RESEARCH

Level 1:

1. Think of different things a Stone Age person might do with the hand axe. How many uses can you name?

2. Based on those uses, what kind of tools do we have today to do the same jobs?

Level 2:

1. Research to learn what historians and scientists believe early humans did with the hand axe? How well did your thoughts (from Level 1 #1) match your research?

2. When did the more skillfully made hand axe first emerge? Was it invented independently from the Oldowan tool? Or did the Oldowan tool evolve into the hand axe?

3. How long did it take for humans to tie a stick to their hand axe? How did that change its use? When was the earliest known use of arrows? Was it before or after adding a stick to the hand axe?

Level 3:

1. There is evidence of the hand axe from many different parts of the world including Asia, Europe, and Africa. Research and consider what that might tell us of either migration with the tool vs. unique and multiple discoveries.

2. Research and discuss Acheulean toolkit. What did it include?

3. Add any other interesting facts that you found in your research.

STEAM ACTIVITIES AND MORE

Level 1

1. Take a hike and look for different rocks: Try to find a flat rock, a round rock, a smooth rock, a rough rock, a gray rock, a brown rock, a colorful rock, a rock with sparkles.

2. Try to break some of the larger rocks you found with another rock. Do any of them break easy? Be sure to wear gloves to protect fingers and use safety goggles to protect eyes from flying stone chips. Parents should demonstrate for younger children.

3. Arrange the rocks in a pattern or by size or shape.

4. Build a rock garden in your flowerbed or yard. Or get creative and give it an arrowhead or other prehistoric theme. If you paint the rocks, consider using natural dyes that early humans might have used such as blueberries or crushed dandelion.

Level 2

1. Take a hike and look for as many different kinds of rock as you can. Then catalog them by type. In your catalog, list characteristics and whether they are hard or soft rocks. Visit your library for a book on local rocks and stones; search online for, "how to identify stones"; or go to https://rockhoundresource.com/how-to-identify-your-rocks-full-guide-with-helpful-tools/.)

2. Choose two soft rocks from your hike and try to shape into an arrowhead or axe (depending on size or the rock). For tips, search online for "how to shape rocks" or visit: https://www.ehow.com/how_4869066_make-stone-arrowheads.html or https://www.wikihow.com/Make-a-Stone-Axe. Note how difficult and challenging it is. Be sure to wear gloves to protect fingers and use safety goggles to protect eyes from flying stone chips. Parents should demonstrate for younger children.

3. Before early humans could pass a new skill down to future generations, they first needed the ability to communicate the lesson. Without using words, teach someone else how to select rocks and make a hand axe or arrowhead. (You can grunt if you want to.)

Level 3

1. Plan to visit a local rock quarry or mine (if open to school tours) or geological science center that offers educational tours. As an alternative, look online for a virtual tour of a quarry or mine. Before your visit, research the quarry or site for what you will learn there and write a report. Then after the tour, update your report with something new that you learned.

2. Make a splash! Choose several rocks of similar mass size but varying shapes and mineral type (thus they can weigh differently). Drop each from the same height into the same container filled with the same amount of water. Measure and analyze the resulting splashes. What might this lesson tell you about inertia and water resistance?

3. Do the same experiment (Level 3 #2) but drop the rocks into sand that is carefully flattened. Measure the impact crater and observe any surrounding changes. How might this help engineers protect us from a meteor strike?

COLORING PAGE

HISTORY UNSCHOOLED: INVENTIONS FROM THE STONE AGE

WORD SEARCH

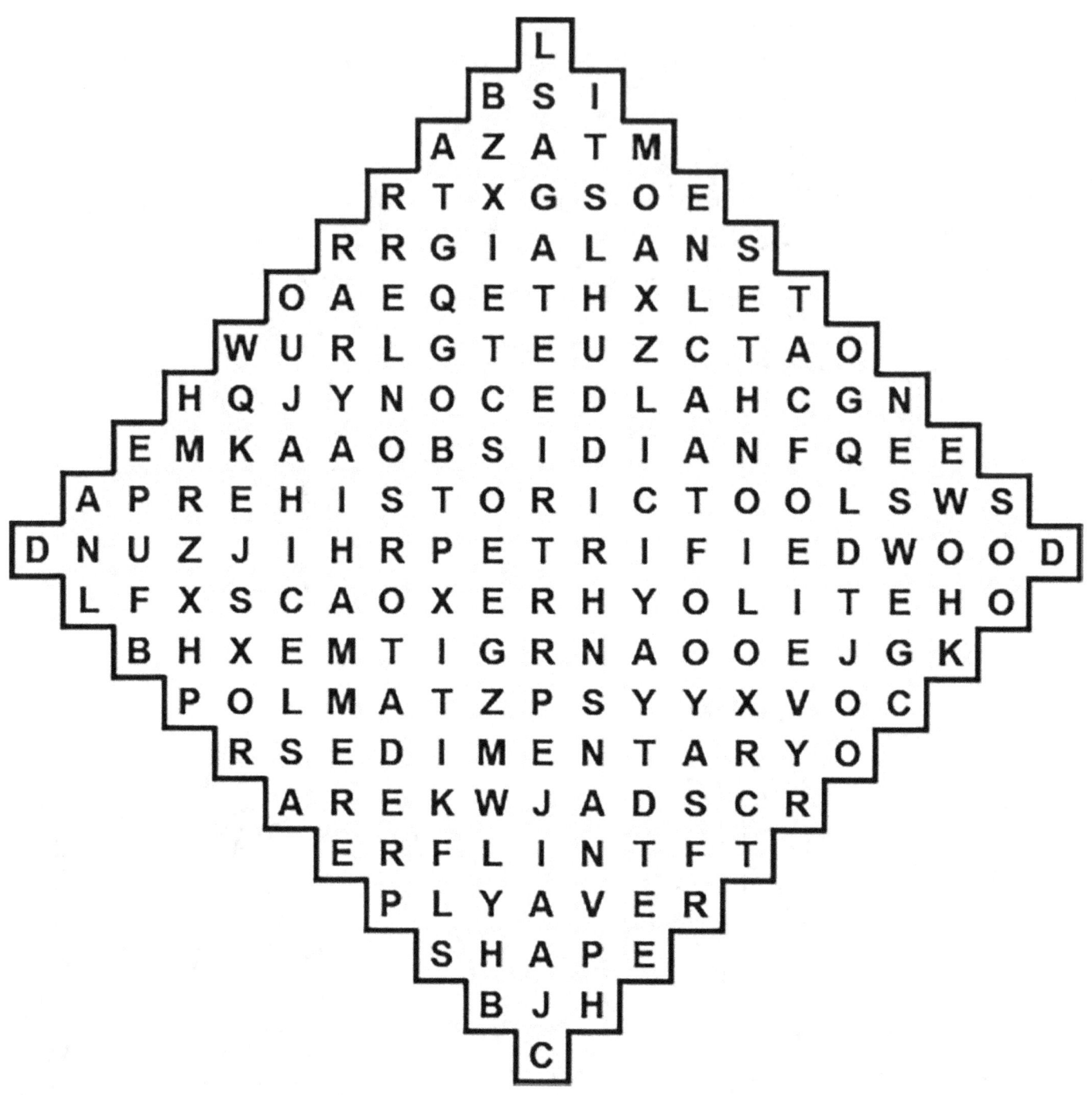

Agate	Flint	Obsidian	Rhyolite
Arrowhead	Hammer	Petrified wood	Sedimentary
Basalt	Hand Axe	Predators	Shape
Chaldecony	Jasper	Prehistoric Tools	Spear
Chert Rock	Limestone	Quartz	Stone Age

INVENTION DISCUSSION PAGE

Name:_____ Date:_____

Invention/Product:_____

Who invented it?_____ When?_____

How does it work?
_____
_____
_____

What problem did it solve?
_____
_____
_____

What was it like before the product was invented? What did people use or do instead?
_____
_____
_____

Who could own it? (Did everyone get to use it? Was it expensive? Was it easy to get?)
_____
_____
_____

Can anyone use this product? What skill was needed to operate it?
_____
_____
_____

Is the product still in use today? How has it changed since its original invention?
_____
_____
_____

FIRE

1 Million BCE

Fire happens naturally, like when lightning strikes a tree or a volcano spills over into a forest. We can't say that one person "invented" fire. But humans did invent a way to purposely start, grow, manage and control fire. That's what truly made them different from animals and primates.

A controlled fire kept early humans warm and safe from predators. Soon, they learned the fire would cook their food. These luxuries may have encouraged other humans to want to gather in clans.

No one really knows where or when the first person learned to make and control fire. Scientists look at fossils, such as traces of wood ash, to find evidence of fire. Some fire fossils were from nature. Scientists look for certain patterns that would indicate control, like a campfire instead of a forest fire.

Early humans probably didn't know how to "make" fire right away. The first fire may have happened by accident, like a lightning strike. Perhaps the human picked up a fiery stick and used it to make a torch. They may have tried to keep the torch going because they didn't know when they'd find another fire. If the fire went out, their protection and warmth went with it.

Someone eventually figured out how to start a new fire. You can rub wooden sticks together to create friction and heat. (Think of Tom Hanks' character in the movie *Cast Away*.) Or you can click two flint and/or pyrite stones together to create a spark. Of course, someone first had to have the idea to do these otherwise seemingly odd actions.

The earliest known evidence of controlled fire is in a cave in South Africa that dates to about 1 million years ago. There are some possibilities dated earlier than that, but not conclusive evidence. If one homo sapien could figure out how to control fire, why couldn't two? Or three? There is evidence of controlled fire by early humans in other parts of Africa and in Asia, Middle East and the Pacific Islands.

Source:

Wikipedia. Control of fire by early humans. Available at: https://en.wikipedia.org/wiki/Control_of_fire_by_early_humans. Accessed May 23, 2023.

READING, WRITING, RESEARCH

Level 1:

1. Talk about ways that fire might have helped early humans?

2. In what ways could fire harm them? What can people do to make sure the fire doesn't hurt them?

3. How do you think early humans figured out that fire can help them?

Level 2:

1. What other ideas or inventions might the advent of fire have sparked for early humans?

2. The Fire Triangle (as fire fighters know) includes the three things needed to create a fire and for the fire to stay alive: oxygen, heat and fuel. If you take any of those away, the fire will go out.

    ➢ Why will a fire go out if you pour water on it?
    ➢ Using the same principle, name three more ways to put out a fire.

Level 3:

1. Research to see where ancient controlled fire sites were located. Use a globe or map of the world to place them. What can you tell about the different places? Were they close together or far apart? What about different times? Does it show that the original discoverers traveled with the knowledge? Or does it show different people may have discovered the same thing in different places?

2. Research and discuss the science behind how flint and pyrite work to create a fire.

STEAM ACTIVITIES AND MORE

Level 1

1. Learn about modern fire safety:
   a. Arrange a visit to your local fire department.
   b. Explore Smokey the Bear's website at https://smokeybear.com/ for age-appropriate videos and activity suggestions to learn Wildfire Prevention, backyard debris burning safety and more.
   c. Show older kids how to check and change fire alarm batteries.
   d. Develop and practice a fire escape plan for your home. Ensure that everyone can get to safety in the event of a fire.

2. Make up a story about a Stone Age family who found or needed fire and show how it helped them. Act out your story with dolls or puppets.

3. Sparky's Fun House is a FREE educational app featuring Sparky the fire dog. It teaches fire safety along with educational carnival games. Search and download it from wherever you get your apps.

Level 2

1. Research Scout-based campfire construction methods using tinder, kindling and fuel. Then practice assembly in your backyard, campsite or other safe place. If your students are scouts, use the opportunity to earn a badge if available.
   a. Girl Scouts: https://my.girlscouts.org/content/dam/girlscouts-vtk2019/local/aid/meetings/B18EB02/How-to-Build-a-Teepee-Fire.pdf.
   b. Boy Scouts: https://scoutingmagazine.org/2021/08/building-campfire-tips/.

2. If your hike to find rocks in Chapter 1 turned up flint or pyrite, use them with an adult's help to make a camp fire. If you only have one (flint or pyrite), you can strike it against a piece of iron or steel to make the spark. Be sure to have a waiting bit of kindling and a ready camp fire already constructed. Discuss how easy or difficult it was to go from spark to camp fire.

3. Learn how to make and use a Firestarter for next time. See Scouting handbook, research online or visit https://www.wikihow.life/Make-a-Fire-Starter. Discuss how early humans might have made fire starting easier with the materials they had on hand. Use your fire to cook a simple meal. For example, roast a hot dog or piece of chicken on a stick. And while you have the fire, don't forget the s'mores!

Level 3

1. Make a fire by rubbing sticks instead of using a match or lighter. (See how at https://www.wikihow.com/Start-a-Fire-with-Sticks or at https://www.modernsurvival.org/make-a-fire-by-rubbing-sticks/). Use natural materials that were handy during the Stone Age to catch and grow the spark. Place it on a waiting piece of bark to safely hold it. Then adults carefully tuck the burning tinder into the base of the constructed campfire.

Remember Safety!

Keep a fire extinguisher or water handy during all fire-related activities. When finished, completely douse the fire and check for hot embers. Make this important step part of the learning process.

2. Imagine you have to travel a long way in the rain. You want to take your fire with you so you don't have to start from scratch when you get there. Devise a safe way to keep your fire dry and alive as you travel.

3. Learn about probability and prediction with the forest fire simulator at http://www.shodor.org/interactivate/activities/DirectableFire/. This uses a rectangular forest and lets you start a fire, determine the speed it spreads and set directional probabilities.

4. Visit https://hessunacademy.com/dragon-fire/ and see which chemicals can change the color of fire. How might this information be useful to firefighters? Be sure to follow all safety precautions as noted in the article to protect eyes, hands and property.

COLORING PAGE

CROSSWORD PUZZLE

Across:

1 Small outdoor blaze for cooking and story telling
3 Petrified or hardened remains of plant or animal
8 Vent in the earth's crust that spews molten rock
10 Key distinction between accidental and deliberate fire
11 Includes Paleolithic and Neolithic eras
12 Creating friction to start a fire (2 words)
13 Stick that carries fire
16 What Smokey the Bear teaches (2 words)
17 Natural fire starter from the sky (2 words)
18 Learn from your local fire department (2 words)
19 Element needed for fire to stay alive
20 Scientific evidence of long ago fire (2 words)

Down:

2 Resistance to motion that can cause heat
4 Delicious dessert after a campfire dinner
5 Character who teaches fire prevention
6 Fred and Wilma; or rocks that can create a spark
7 Bipedal primates that refers to humans (2 words, Latin)
9 What happens when flint strikes iron
14 When people attain social development
15 Something you make to help start a fire (2 words)

INVENTION DISCUSSION PAGE

Name:_____ Date:_____

Invention/Product:_____

Who invented it?_____When?_____

How does it work?
_____
_____
_____

What problem did it solve?
_____
_____
_____

What was it like before the product was invented? What did people use or do instead?
_____
_____
_____

Who could own it? (Did everyone get to use it? Was it expensive? Was it easy to get?)
_____
_____
_____

Can anyone use this product? What skill was needed to operate it?
_____
_____
_____

Is the product still in use today? How has it changed since its original invention?
_____
_____
_____

CLOTHING

500,000 to 100,000 BCE

Anthropologists are not able to pin a date on the invention of clothing. Some believe clothing happened out of necessity when humans first started to migrate northward into colder climates, which was between 50,000 and 100,000 years ago.

Others use the evolution of human body lice to help date the invention of clothing. That's because the body louse cannot live outside of clothing. Since the body louse is about 107,000 years old, the theory says that clothing has to be at least that old.

Still other anthropologists believe clothing could go as far back as 500,000 years ago. That is when Neanderthals roamed Europe while *homo bodoensis* remained in Africa. That was over 100,000 years before the earliest known *homo sapiens* appeared.

Early humans used animal skins and plants to help cover their bodies when cold. They may have draped themselves with the furs from the animals they killed. It probably didn't take long to figure out how to tie them on with long grasses, vines and strips of animal hide. Later, they decorated their clothing with other natural materials like shells and feathers.

There is evidence of bone awl tools dating back 84,000 years. These would have been used to pierce soft materials like leather. This indicates early humans will have learned tanning methods.

Simple needles made from animal bone were evident about 30,000 years ago, indicating they had eventually learned to sew. And woven fabrics dating to about 6,500 to 6,700 BCE have been found at a Neolithic era archeological site in Turkey.

Sources:

- Bellis, Mary. "The History of Clothing." ThoughtCo, Aug. 27, 2020, https://www.thoughtco.com/history-of-clothing-1991476

- Wikipedia. History of clothing and textiles. Available at: https://en.wikipedia.org/wiki/History_of_clothing_and_textiles

- Priest, Tyler (26 January 2018). "How shall we save the planet? The Wizard and the Prophet Charles C. Mann Alfred A. Knopf, 2018. 629 pp". Science. 359 (6374): 399. doi:10.1126/science. aar2447. ISSN 0036-8075. S2CID 13685833.

- Gilligan, Ian (March 2010). "The Prehistoric Development of Clothing: Archaeological Implications of a Thermal Model". Journal of Archaeological Method and Theory. 17 (1): 15-80. doi:10.1007/s10816-009-9076-x. JSTOR 25653129. S2CID 143004288.

- Rast-Eicher, A., Karg, S., & Bender Jørgensen, L. (2021). The use of local fibres for textiles at Neolithic Çatalhöyük. Antiquity, 95(383), 1129-1144. doi:10.15184/aqy.2021.89

READING, WRITING, RESEARCH

Level 1:

1. Read a book about animals that lived during the ice age. Which animal furs do you think the people used for their clothing?

2. What other natural things could people use to make the first clothing?

3. What natural materials were used to decorate the first clothing? Why do you think they decorated their clothing?

Level 2:

1. Discuss how the invention of sewing might have changed people's wardrobe.

2. Research and explain why early humans stretched their hides. (See Level 3 #1 on page 31.)

3. Research "earliest evidence of shoes" and see what you find. How long did it take for humans to add shoes to their wardrobe? What materials did they use for shoes?

Level 3:

1. Research and discuss the evolution of clothing throughout the Stone Age (up to the start of the Bronze Age). Explain how, when and why the clothing changed over time.

2. Research the various theories on when clothing was invented. Which theory do you think is true? Debate your choice with someone who disagrees. Research online to learn about debate methods.

STEAM ACTIVITIES AND MORE

Level 1

1. Learn the process of weaving using strips of construction paper. Use different colors to make a pattern. Make a frame for your design.

2. Have a fashion show. Design a clothing line (for yourself, a doll or a puppet) using real natural elements (such as wool, palm leaves or tall grasses), or imitation products like faux fur or leather. You can also use animal print fabrics to symbolize fur. Use early methods to attach the clothing (no sewing machines or modern threads allowed.)

3. Decorate your clothing line with sticks, stones, shells, feathers, or chicken bones.

Level 2

1. Design a clothing line as above. (Level 1: #2) Classify your designs for different members of the social hierarchy (the leader, the fire keeper, the hunters, the gatherers, etc.) Explain those classifications during your fashion show.

2. Write a story about the invention of clothing and how it was created from necessity. Include a scene where the clan leader added something special to his clothing to show that he (or she) is the boss.

3. Find some animal fibers (such as wool) and plant fibers (such as cotton). Touch them. Look at them close up with a magnifying glass or microscope if you have one. Add in manmade fibers such as nylon, polyester or acrylic. How are each of these materials the same and how are they different?

4. Practice hand sewing with a large needle and yarn on canvas or faux leather. Make something simple such as a satchel or shopping tote bag. (See also practice activity on page 34.)

5. Learn to knit or crochet. Counting stitches is important so your design is even. Make something small, such as a dish cloth, or larger, like a scarf.

Level 3

1. Make a square frame from sticks and natural materials. Tie a piece of faux leather or wool to stretch it. (Pretend it's a fresh animal hide.)

2. Use a sharp rock to chisel an awl out of a beef or pork bone. (This is a tool with a flat end on one side and a point on the other, which you can hammer to pierce a hole in leather.)

3. Test your awl. Design something useful that you can make from leather or vinyl and hold together with yarn or string, such as a satchel or sitting mat. Use your awl tool to make holes along the edges. Then thread string or yarn through the holes to "sew" your pieces together.

COLORING PAGE

WORD SEARCH

```
D E C O R A T I V E S T O N E S S
S Q E T A M I L C D L O C N Y Q L
H U M A N B O D Y L O U S E T Z W
I Y F W G K H I J R R P H E M A A
X T E H A U K R O W E D I H D L X
M C L I M R R L B M H B O N E S N
N S D E C Z N N S W T R Q W F M R
A E E R R Y J I W Z A Z O H E A N
D A E A W S L J K W E O U Q A G E
O S N R G Z F J S S L U G D T X C
R H G C S S A R G L L A T S H S E
N E N H N O Z X C L S A W W E E S
M L I Y G N I H T O L C M N R I S
E L W E X L B K X D G S I I S N I
N S E X B I J G H S X V U J N X T
T T S I G O L O P O R H T N A A Y
T A N N I N G V I L D J F R K H J
```

Adornment	Clothing	Hierarchy	Sewing Needle
AnimalSkin	Cold Climate	Human Body Louse	Tall Grass
Anthropologist	Decorative Stones	Leather	Tanning
Awl	Feathers	Necessity	Vines
Bones	Hide work	Seashells	Wool

COLOR, THEN SEW!

Retrace or glue page onto card stock for easier sewing. Sew along the dotted outline to complete the picture.

34 | JJ CARROLL

INVENTION DISCUSSION PAGE

Name:_____ Date:_____

Invention/Product:_____

Who invented it?_____ When?_____

How does it work?
_____
_____
_____

What problem did it solve?
_____
_____
_____

What was it like before the product was invented? What did people use or do instead?
_____
_____
_____

Who could own it? (Did everyone get to use it? Was it expensive? Was it easy to get?)
_____
_____
_____

Can anyone use this product? What skill was needed to operate it?
_____
_____
_____

Is the product still in use today? How has it changed since its original invention?
_____
_____
_____

WRITTEN COMMUNICATION

70,000 BCE

We usually think of the oldest written languages as Sumerian cuneiform and Egyptian hieroglyphs, which date to around 3,000 BCE. But, these language didn't just emerge from nothing. Written communication is much, much older than that.

A "rock cupule" is an artificial hole, shaped like a half-sphere, carved into rocks. They look like someone dipped a ping pong ball into wet cement to make a depression. But, these rock cupules were made by hammering a hard rounded rock into a softer flat rock surface.[1]

These depressions show up on every continent except Antarctica. They are found on vertical, horizontal and even sloped surfaces. Some are estimated to be over 400,000 years old.

Some scientists believe they are a form of communication while others do not. It's possible they have different meanings and purposes. For example, they may have served travelers by marking territories or locations. If someone stamped holes in the rocks and someone else understood the holes, that would be communication.

In 2002, archaeologists discovered a series of geometric shapes (including rock cupules) carved into the walls of the sub-Saharan Blombos Cave. This is currently the oldest known rock art, dating to about 70,000 years.

Most of us think of Stone Age communications in the form of cave art. La Ferrassie Cave in southwest France is known to be a Neanderthal cave that contains petroglyphs, which date to about 60,000 BCE.[2]

Painted cave art, like those found in the cave at Lascaux, France, date as far back as 17,000 years ago. Still other cave paintings have been dated to 40,000 years ago. That doesn't mean such art didn't happen earlier than that. Paint simply doesn't last as long as rock.

Canadian paleoanthropologist and rock art researcher Genevieve von Petzinger believes there are patterns or abstract geometric symbols found in many of the cave paintings.[4] She believes these symbols may help us unlock an early form of graphic communication.

Once humans began settling in large communities and trading with each other, a standard form of communication was necessary. Sumerians created cuneiform around 3,500 BCE.

At first, it was in the form of pictures.[5] But soon, more detailed symbols were needed to communicate what pictures could not. The root word of cuneiform is the Latin cuneus, which means wedge. They used a wedge shaped point to depress into clay in different ways to form the symbols that represented words.

Egyptians also developed a writing method called hieroglyphics ('sacred carvings'). They may have seen cuneiform during trade and came up with their own system some time before 3,150 BCE.

Written communications was a game changer in trade, record keeping, war and peace, and other events that required someone to help negotiate with leaders of a distant land.

Sources:

1. *Wikipedia.com. Rock cupule. Available at https://en.wikipedia.org/wiki/Rock_cupule.*

2. *Ancient History Lists. Top 10 Oldest Art Ever Discovered (ancienthistorylists.com). Available at https://www.ancienthistorylists.com/pre-history/top-10-oldest-art-ever-discovered/. Accessed March 20, 2023.*

3. *Wikipedia. History of Communications. Available at: https://en.wikipedia.org/wiki/History_of_communication. Accessed April 5, 2023.*

4. *NewScientists.com. Code hidden in Stone Age art may be the root of human writing. Available at: https://www.newscientist.com/article/mg23230990-700-in-search-of-the-very-first-coded-symbols/. Accessed March 20, 2023.*

5. *WorldHistory.com. Cuneiform. Available at: https://www.worldhistory.org/cuneiform/. Accessed May 25, 2023.*

READING, WRITING, RESEARCH

Level 1:
1. Why do you think drawn images came before the alphabet?
2. How can you tell people what you're thinking through art?
3. What do the symbols below mean? How do you know what they mean?

Level 2:
1. Search online for these phrases to find virtual tours and videos:
   - Cave of Lascaux (France)
   - Blombos Cave (South Africa)
   - "Ice Age Cave Art: Unlocking the Mysteries Behind These Markings" by Nat Geo Live.
2. Research the Cosquer Cave near Marseilles on the Mediterranean Sea. Note that it has paintings and engravings that span from 27,000 and 19,000 years ago. That means even when the newest art was created, the older art was already ancient. (We consider the Roman civilization to be ancient and that was only 2,000 years ago. The age difference for the art inside the same cave is 8,000 years!) How do you think the newer humans reacted when they saw the ancient art? Did the art style change from older to newer?
3. Math is considered the "universal language." Why do you think that is? Look at the symbols for plus, minus, times and divide. How do those symbols look in China? Russia? Germany? Spain? Argentina?

Level 3:
1. Research the history of international symbolism and discuss why it works.
2. Learn about Egyptian Hieroglyphs. See how letters are assigned to the different animal and people symbols. See also how the positions of the symbols (eating, sleeping, etc.) can change the meaning. How easy or difficult is it to master? Review:
   a. Discover Egypt: Ancient Egyptian Hieroglyphic Writing. Available at: https://discoveringegypt.com/egyptian-hieroglyphic-writing/egyptian-hieroglyphic-alphabet/
   b. Wikipedia: List of Egyptian hieroglyphs. Available at: https://en.wikipedia.org/wiki/List_of_Egyptian_hieroglyphs.

STEAM ACTIVITIES AND MORE

Level 1

1. Using sidewalk chalk on a rough outside surface, such as sidewalk or driveway, have students draw a picture to "tell" about a particular event they'd like to remember. If you have multiple students, have them do their pictures in secret and try to interpret each other's drawings.

2. Think of the symbol question (Level 1 #3) on page 38. Drive around and see how many more symbols you can find. Make a list of all of them. Make up a new symbol to tell others something common but important.

3. Research and list as many math symbols as you can. What do they all mean?

4. Create a pattern of cupules in plaster wall art. Search online for "DIY plaster wall art" to find a video or instructions. Vary the sizes of different spherical objects to make the depressions. Paint or label the cupule sizes (small, medium, large) or measure them in centimeters and again in inches.

Level 2

1. Create a timeline of the Paleolithic era. Research major cave art discoveries and show where they fit on the timeline.
- ➢ Australian Aboriginal rock paintings
- ➢ Cave paintings at Chauvet, France.
- ➢ The Cussac cave in France
- ➢ The cave art of Lascaux, France
- ➢ The cave paintings at Le Portal, France.

2. Do the cupules craft in Level 1 #4 above, but try to make sense of your cupules or create a particular message.

3. Tell about an event using only common emoji symbols from a phone or tablet.

Level 3

1. Do the cupules craft in Level 1: #4. Then find the volume of each cupule depression: Use your math resource for equation information or visit https://www.wikihow.com/Calculate-the-Volume-of-a-Sphere.

2. Play Pictionary with abstract nouns. An abstract noun is a noun that doesn't exist in the physical world. You cannot touch it, see it, smell it, hear it or taste it. For example,"determination," "speed" and "luck" are abstract nouns.

DRAW CAVE ART ANIMALS

Can you draw these images?

MAKE A SECRET ALPHABET

These are real symbols found in caves all over the world. Assign each symbol with a letter, sound or word to make up a language. Then write a secret note to someone else.

Aviform	Circle	Claviform	Cordiform	Crosshatch	Cruciform
Cupules	Dot	Finger fluting	Flabelliform	Half Circle	Line
Negative Hand	Open Angle	Oval	Pectiform	Penniform	Positive Hand
Quadrangle	Reniform	Scalariform	Serpentiform	Spiral	Tectiform

INVENTION DISCUSSION PAGE

Name:_____ Date:_____

Invention/Product:_____

Who invented it?_____ When?_____

How does it work?
_____
_____
_____

What problem did it solve?
_____
_____
_____

What was it like before the product was invented? What did people use or do instead?
_____
_____
_____

Who could own it? (Did everyone get to use it? Was it expensive? Was it easy to get?)
_____
_____
_____

Can anyone use this product? What skill was needed to operate it?
_____
_____
_____

Is the product still in use today? How has it changed since its original invention?
_____
_____
_____

MEDICINE AND FIRST AID

60,000- 31 000 BCE

Famous anthropologist Margaret Meade is often quoted as having said that a healed femur is the earliest sign of civilization. Without modern x-rays, early man might not know a bone was broken. But the injured person would clearly need help – perhaps for many days or weeks. A fractured bone needs time to heal and a person with a broken arm or leg would need food and protection while waiting for it to mend. Without a helper, they might fall victim to the weather, starvation or animal attack.

Early humans saw others get sick and die. They also saw people get hurt and live. Those observations could show them ways they might help. Like keeping the limb immobile with a branch. Or eating certain plants when they felt sick.

There is some evidence that humans used mallow and yarrow as medicines about 60,000 years ago.[1] Mallow has a gooey substance inside that can sooth a sore throat. The juice from yarrow leaves has been used to heal wounds.

The earliest evidence of complicated surgery was an amputation from about 31,000 years ago. The person lived another 7 to 9 years after the surgery.[2]

Trepanation is a form of surgery where a hole is drilled in the skull to relieve pressure on the brain or to investigate and treat head wounds. There is evidence of trepanation as far back as 12,000 BCE. In fact it was so common that out of 120 skulls found in one burial site in France (circa 6,500 BCE), 40 of them had trepanation holes.[2]

Sources:

1. *Wikipedia. History of Surgery. Available at: https://en.wikipedia.org/wiki/History_of_surgery. Accessed March 20, 2023.*
2. *Medical News Today. What was medicine like in prehistoric times? Available at: https://www.medicalnewstoday.com/articles/323556#medications. Accessed March 20, 2023.*

READING, WRITING, RESEARCH

Level 1:
1. Learn about healing flowers and herbs that grow near where you live. You can find information at your local library or search online. You can also ask an expert of healing herbs if you know one. Draw or cut out pictures and paste on pages. Write the names next to each picture. Make a book with your pages.
2. Think about all the things that can hurt a person if left alone in the woods without help. What will a person need to stay healthy while waiting for the leg to heal?
3. If you were a Stone Age doctor, what items would you carry with you wherever you went?

Level 2:
1. Look up flowers and herbs that grow near where you live. Make a chart of the names, what they look like, and how they can help you. For example, feverfew (a small daisy-like flower with white petals and a yellow center) can lower a fever.
2. Even long accepted information can be wrong. Some say that Margaret Meade never actually said that a healed femur was the earliest sign of civilization. And Hippocrates never wrote, "Let food be thy medicine and medicine be thy food" even though everyone said he did. (Search both quotes online with the added term "misquote" and see results.) Review the lesson on Research Skills (page 04). Discuss how and why misinformation can happen and why primary sources are important.

Level 3:
1. Research and discuss (or write) how Stone Age people may have discovered the uses for each medicine. How might they have known that plants have healing properties in the first place? Which were the first plants used as medicine and how do today's scientists know that?
2. Research medicinal plants that grew in Africa and Europe during the last Ice Age. What were they used for? Consider how Stone Age people performed surgeries such as amputations and trepanations without the benefit of sterile environment or anesthetics. Are there any plants they might have used to help in either case?
3. Research Stone Age life expectancies and infant mortality rates. "Mortality rate" refers to deaths per thousand. A high mortality rate is bad and a low mortality rate is good. Compare with today's life expectancy and infant mortality rates.
4. Choose and research any present-day indigenous peoples (Australian Aborigine, American Indian, Alaskan Natives, isolated African Peoples, etc.,) who may still use ancient methods of medicine. How do their methods compare with what we think we know about Stone Age people? Who administers medicine and how does that person get the job? What are their success rates?

STEAM ACTIVITIES AND MORE

Level 1

1. Go for a hike to collect the flowers and herbs you learned about on page 45, Level 1: #1. Put them in small jars and label their names.

2. Make flashcards of those useful herbs. Draw a picture and write the name of each flower and herb you collected. Add to your flashcards over time as you learn more. Practice remembering them so you know what they are when you see them.

3. Blindfold students and sit in a circle. Pass around different herbs. (Make sure they are edible first.) Each student should describe the herbs using their senses – how does it feel, smell, taste, etc.? Can you guess which one you have without looking?

Level 2

1. Take a first aid class as a family. Visit https://www.redcross.org/take-a-class or check your local area.
   a. Practice techniques on each other or on a doll.
   b. Create and stock a first aid kit based on what you learned.
   c. Discuss what a Stone Age first aid kit might contain.

2. Go for a hike to collect local medicinal flowers and herbs. Plant an herb garden with your collection. Research each one separately for best planting tips. Find smooth rocks and paint them to label your garden.

3. Medicines have to enter your blood stream in order to be effective. Pills need to dissolve in your stomach before that can happen. Collect different over- the-counter (non-prescription) medicines in your house (with a parent's permission and guidance). Mix it up! Collect coated and uncoated, capsules, alka-seltzer, powders, etc. Add two tablespoons of an acid (lemon juice or vinegar) to one cup of water for each test. Time each as you dissolve it in the water mixture. Record the results.

Level 3

1. Learn and understand the difference between urgent care and emergency care. Make a chart with different medical situations and consider if each is okay for an urgent care center or if you should call 911. Examples: hurt ankle in a fall, cut finger with scissors, burned finger on stove, sunburn, severe headache, dizziness, passed out, chest pain, uncontrollable hiccups.

    a. Learn where your nearest urgent care center is and have a family drive to find it in case of future need.

    b. A true medical emergency is when someone feels their life or a bodily function is in danger. In case of a true medical emergency, call 911.

2. Create an emergency action plan. Search online for "How to react in an emergency" for helpful and memorable tips. Here are two results:
https://blogs.cdc.gov/publichealthmatters/2016/11/this-is-your-brain-on-emergencies/
and https://www.wikihow.com/Handle-an-Emergency-Situation.

3. Research more deeply and create a medicinal catalog with the plants you collected. Draw and describe each specimen and include information about where and when it grows, best time to harvest, parts of the plants needed for medicinal uses, and how to use it (i.e., brew into a tea, crush in mortar and pestle to make a topical paste, or mix with other ingredients to digest like a medicine, etc.)

WARNING:

Never self-medicate without discussing with your doctor first. Some medicinal herbs can interact badly with, or lessen the effectiveness of, other medicines you may take.

COLORING PAGE

Medical Mixup

Unscramble the medicine chart. Draw a line from each plant name to its correct use as a medicine.

Chamomile
Anthemis nobilis

Feverfew
Chrysanthemum parthenium

Foxglove
Digitalis purpurea

Lady's Mantle
Ichemilla vulgaris

Lavender
Lavandula angustifolia

Marrow
Malva

Pennyroyal
Mentha pulegium

Poppy
Papaver rhoeas

Rosemary
Rosmarinus officinalis

Sage
Salvia officinalis

Wintergreen
Pyrola minor

Yarrow
Achillea millefolium

Regulates heart rhythm

Used to treat headaches, epilepsy and poor circulation. Also makes a good mouthwash.

Soothes pain and inflammation

Helps mouth and throat irritation and dry cough

Use topically on wounds or as a natural antiseptic in mouthwash

The petals are helpful in treating asthma, bronchitis, whooping cough and angina

Remedy for laryngitis, tonsillitis and sore throats. Also sweeten with honey to make a mild laxative

For migraines and fevers

Ease headaches and colicky belly pains

Use on minor cuts or as a medicine to speed recovery from sever bruising

Stops bleeding

Reduce stress

WARNING:

Never self-treat with medicine. Talk to your doctor first about any allergies you have and other medicines you take that may have harmful interactions with certain herbs.

Source:

National Library of Medicine. List of Herbs in the NLM Herb Garden. Available at: https://www.nlm.nih.gov/about/herbgarden/list.html. Accessed March 21, 2023.

INVENTION DISCUSSION PAGE

Name:_____ Date:_____

Invention/Product:_____

Who invented it?_____ When?_____

How does it work?
_____
_____
_____

What problem did it solve?
_____
_____
_____

What was it like before the product was invented? What did people use or do instead?
_____
_____
_____

Who could own it? (Did everyone get to use it? Was it expensive? Was it easy to get?)
_____
_____
_____

Can anyone use this product? What skill was needed to operate it?
_____
_____
_____

Is the product still in use today? How has it changed since its original invention?
_____
_____
_____

POTTERY AND BASKETS

16,000 – 4,000 BCE

Stone Age people would have first used animal skins as a carrying vessel long before using more inventive sources. Merely killing an animal and removing its bladder would reveal the grand idea of holding and transporting water. It wouldn't have been long for humans to replicate the organ with animal skins to use as an important part of their traveling luggage.

More skilled creations came as the needs to carry and hold products increased.

It's easy to tell that wet clay can be molded into shapes, but it either took a long time to figure out how to harden it for use, or perhaps early results didn't survive well over the years. Evidence shows the oldest use of clay pots for cooking and food storage are from the Neolithic era about 16,000 to 18,000 years ago.[1, 2]

The introduction of baskets predates woven cloth. In 2021, archaeologists found in a cave in Israel what is believed to be the oldest known, well-preserved, woven basket.[3] Researchers determined it is about 10,500 years old. It is large and has a lid, but not much else is known about it yet, including the plant used to make it. The researchers said it took two people to complete the intricate weave.

That alone tells us it was a learned skill that may have been handed down for some time. So the general age of basketry could be much older still. The dry climate and undisturbed nature of the cave helped to preserve it. Otherwise, the straw material would not hold up well over time, which makes this old basket a rare find.

Sources:

1. *History.com. Stone Age. Available at: https://www.history.com/topics/prehistory/stone-age. Accessed March 21, 2023.*
2. *Smithsonian National Museum of Natural History. What Does it Mean to be Human? Available at: https://humanorigins.si.edu/evidence/behavior/carrying-storing/oldest-pottery. Accessed March 21, 2023.*
3. *Jerusalem Post. The Oldest Basket in the World. Available at: https://www.jpost.com/archaeology/oldest-woven-basket-in-the-world-found-in-israel-dates-back-10000-years-662183. Accessed March 24, 2023.*

READING, WRITING, RESEARCH

Level 1:

1. How do you think weaving baskets changed the way people made clothing?

2. When the first humans appeared, they were nomads. That means they traveled from place to place without a permanent home. When the Ice Age started to end, people found places where some grains grew wild. So they stopped moving around and stayed in one place. Why do you think clay pots were invented after people started to live in one place instead of traveling all the time?

3. Which do you think is easier to make: a clay pot or a basket? Why do you think clay pots were invented before baskets?

Level 2:

1. Look up how much water modern doctors say humans need each day to survive. Do you think that's the same as Stone Age humans? How would they have accessed that much water while traveling?

2. Research the earliest evidence of making cord or rope. How might that have led to basket-weaving?

Level 3:

1. The last ice age ended nearly 2,000 years before the oldest known basket's supposed age. How might the change in climate make basket weaving possible?

2. Food preservation methods like smoking meats and fermenting milk also date to the Paleolithic era.[1] How might the inventions of pottery and baskets along with food preservation change their eating habits? How might changes in eating habits affect their health?

Sources:

1. *Nummer, Brian A., PhD. National Center for Home Food Preservation. 2002. Historical Origins of Food Preservation. Available at: https://nchfp.uga.edu/publications/nchfp/factsheets/food_pres_hist.html. Accessed March 24, 2023.*

STEAM ACTIVITIES AND MORE

Level 1

1. Parents search online for "DIY loom for kids" or "simple weaving projects." Or make up your own using fabric, construction paper or whatever you have on hand.

2. Use play dough, modeling clay or backyard mud/clay to create household items like cooking pots, eating plate, spoon or pitcher.

3. Take a local pottery class. If possible, make something that might have been used during the Stone Age, such as a clay pot with lid to hold food.

Level 2

1. Look up "the chemistry of pottery," or go to https://edu.rsc.org/feature/the-chemistry-of-pottery/2020245. Discuss why some clays can be hardened for pots while other kinds can't.

2. Collect willow branches in your neighborhood and look up how to weave a simple bowl or basket. If you can't access willow branches, try another long skinny, bendable source such as palm leaves. Look up "DIY basket weaving" or take a basket weaving class.

3. Update or expand your fashion line (from clothing chapter) using the added skill of weaving.

Level 3

1. Search online for "how did they make pottery in the Stone Age," for further learning. Then search on "make pottery from clay in my backyard" or "diy pottery clay" to try it for yourself. For an added challenge, design and build a simple potter's wheel to make a uniform shape out of turned clay. Watch the building of a potter's wheel, Stone Age style, at: https://youtu.be/Gqhxe_pL6Ws.

2. Stone Age people first smoked meats in the mouths of caves. Research survival methods of smoking meat and replicate it in your backyard with fresh fish. As an alternative, search online for a fermented food recipe. Then try it! Examples include fermented cheese, sauerkraut or pickles.

3. Research and learn the geological and chemical sciences behind clay and hardening it into something useful. For example, search on "the chemistry of pottery" or "geology of clay." Teach a family member what you learned.

CROSSWORD PUZZLE

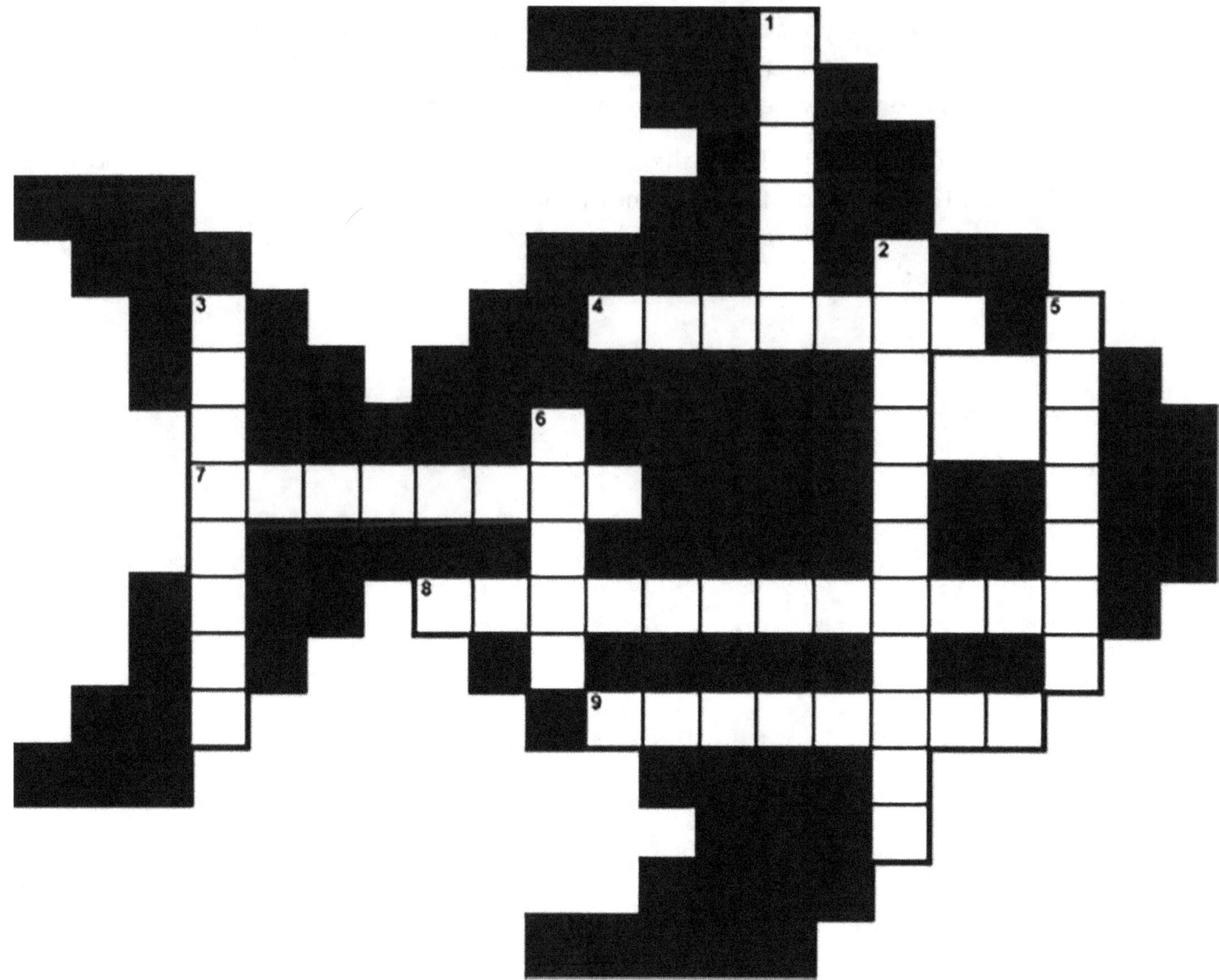

Down:
1. How early man preserved fish and meats (past tense)
2. Levels of family or clan members who handed down learned skills
3. Keep food from spoiling
5. How early man made cheese
6. Method used to make a basket

Across:
4. Internal organ that can hold liquid
7. How early man preserved grapes (2 words, past tense)
8. Complex human society
9 First used for cooking and food storage about 16,000 BCE (plural)

WORD SEARCH

```
O H P R E S E R V A T I O N L S O
A R R E D D A L B A S R U H V L J
D T C G J P F Z E Y K I C Q L A T
S N I K S L A M I N A N T W L I R
Q G C C O F D K W R A I J U F R A
C D N H X E I F F R U P G F L E N
U I X I K C S V B R O G E J A T S
U L V O V B L W F T A R T H X A P
C A M I B A O D T G M P K W C M O
L S U G L L E E E E H U V L R S R
A S W K L I R W N S R T H U N U T
Y T B I R Y Z T M L T R U D V O F
P E W D J X A A U J P I Q T S R O
O K L N D T E T T R R D Y O X B O
T S A V I A W W F I S A L T O I D
S A R O G G W K C O O K I N G F S
A B N N L L I K S D E N R A E L T
```

Animal Skins
Baskets
Bladder
Civilization
Clay Pots

Cooking
Dried Fruit
Fermentation
Fibrous Materials
Flax

Preservation
Learned Skill
Luggage
Pottery
Putrid

Salt
Smoked Meat
Transport Foods
Weaving
Willow Branch

MAZE

Help the mouse find the basket of grain.

INVENTION DISCUSSION PAGE

Name:_____ Date:_____

Invention/Product:_____

Who invented it?_____ When?_____

How does it work?
_____
_____
_____

What problem did it solve?
_____
_____
_____

What was it like before the product was invented? What did people use or do instead?
_____
_____
_____

Who could own it? (Did everyone get to use it? Was it expensive? Was it easy to get?)
_____
_____
_____

Can anyone use this product? What skill was needed to operate it?
_____
_____
_____

Is the product still in use today? How has it changed since its original invention?
_____
_____
_____

AGRICULTURE

8,500 BCE

The Neolithic transition from hunting and gathering to agriculture and settlement was the beginning of the end of the Stone Age. This period saw the first intentional planting of edible flora rather than scouting for foods, starting around 8,500 BCE.

The agricultural revolution is so named because it transformed not only the way people ate but also the way people lived. Instead of being nomads on a varied diet, they now lived and worked in villages, sharing with their neighbors the work of cultivating fields, harvesting and storing grains and protecting their food supply from wild beasts.

Humans were no longer constantly on the move. They had less trouble catching their food and they ate easier-to-chew food as well as a lesser variety of foods. This caused an evolutionary shift in the physicality of humans giving them smaller muscles, smaller faces, jaws and teeth, and more periodontal disease.[1]

As the villages grew to cities, it was clear that not all jobs were directly related to the growth of food. The result led to refined social hierarchies and the creation of wealth.

The Stone Age ends with the discovery of bronze (about 3,800 BCE). Before the Bronze Age began, humans had long since become proficient at cultivating grains and were a few hundred years away from discovery of bread and fermented dough.

Sources:

1. Martin-Merino, Mario. 2021. The Neolithic Revolution: agriculture, sedentary lifestyle and its consequences. Available at: https://www.cambridge.org/engage/api-gateway/coe/assets/orp/resource/item/60e1c1255cb3f6e5a99224e0/original/the-neolithic-revolution-agriculture-sedentary-lifestyle-and-its-consequences.pdf Accessed March 26, 2023.

READING, WRITING, RESEARCH

Level 1:

1. Why do you think people wanted to grow food instead of hunt for it in the woods? How did that make life better for them?

2. Villages grew grains to be shared by everyone. How do you think they kept the grain safe and dry from rain? Think of different ways the people might have shared the grains so it was fair?

3. If barns weren't invented yet, where do you think the farm animals lived? Why do you think that?

Level 2:

1. What do you think of the Neolithic Agricultural Revolution? Would you rather experience the dangers of the hunter-gatherer lifestyle? Or do you prefer living in protected cities with a ruler, different classes of people, and a specific job to do? Explain your choice and why you think so.

2. Visit and discuss different elements on the Timeline of Agriculture and Food Technology at: https://en.wikipedia.org/wiki/Timeline_of_agriculture_and_food_technology#External_links.

   a. What is the oldest line on the timeline?
   b. What was the first planted food mentioned on the timeline? Why do you think this might have been the first food planted?
   c. What was the last item on the timeline before the Bronze Age?
   d. Notice that animals are included on the Stone Age farm. Which were the first farm animals? Why do you think they were first?

3. On the timeline in #2, you'll see that oats had been "processed" (ground with a pestle) 26,000 years before the invention of bread (30,600 to 4,000 BCE). If they weren't using the ground oats for bread, what do you think they did with it? Research to see if you can find an answer.

Level 3:

1. Research the history of money and bartering. Discuss how the shift to agriculture may have created the phenomenon of wealth.

2. Animals like sabretooth tigers and woolly mammoths went extinct around the time that humans shifted from hunter/gatherer to agriculture. Research to find out if these events are connected, and if so, how.

3. Scientists disagree on whether farming caused people to settle into villages or if living in villages caused them to invent farming. Research the first known settlements and decide which you think is right and why? Have a formal debate with someone who disagrees. Topics to help research:

    a. GöbekliTepe
    b. Natufians and Epipaleolithic people
    c. Eastern Fertile Crescent
    d. Ancient Levant

STEAM ACTIVITIES AND MORE

Level 1

1. Find a simple recipe that uses a mortar and pestle to grind an ingredient. Then have fun making it! For example you can grind raw nuts to make a nut butter, berries to make a fruit spread, beans to make a bean dip, or avocados to make guacamole.

2. Set up a pretend store of pantry ingredients. But instead of using money, customers have to trade something to get what you're selling.

3. Use grains as seeds and plant them in a glass jar so you can watch them grow. (Parents search on "homeschool activity for seed germination" to find instructions and pictures.)

Level 2

1. Use a mortar and pestle to grind whole oats into oat flour. How difficult was it? What does it look and feel like? How much whole grain do you need to grind to make a useful batch of flour?

2. Milk, butter and honey were all first enjoyed during the Stone Age. Use them (add water if needed) to invent an oatcake recipe with your whole and ground oats. Test and record your recipe with precise measurements.
   - **a.** For added challenge, use a campfire (with a parent's help) instead of modern oven to cook them.
   - **b.** Then taste and discuss the flavor, texture, health benefits and difficulty in making them, against alternative foods available during the time.
   - **c.** Do oatcakes travel well? Save a few oatcakes for next day or next several days and see how well they age.
   - **d.** If they crumble, modify the recipe to help them stand up better. What happens to the flavor/edibility if you do? Adjust your recorded recipe as needed.

3. Oat porridge (oatmeal) is another food that later Stone Age likely ate. But this requires a bowl and spoon which haven't been invented yet. Using only natural materials, find a way to serve and eat oatmeal.

Level 3

1. Create a small garden where you grow a type of grain (wheat, oats, barley, rye or corn). If space is limited, do your best with what you have, like use a planter box on the patio. If necessary, look for community garden space. Research what grows best in your area and how to grow it. Research and discuss soil needs, fertilizers, tools, etc. Compare how today's products differed from Stone Age availabilities.

2. Research and determine how much land it would take to grow enough grain to feed the village, town or city you live in for one year? What factors might affect the answer?

COLOR AND LEARN

Fill in the missing stages.

There are six stages for growing wheat.

Seedling	The first leaves emerge from the soil.
Tiller	New shoots grow from the root of the plant. Each tiller can grow its own stalk and seed head. The number of tillers determines the yield of the plant.
Jointing	The stalk forms a second "joint" from which the plant telescopes upward. The smaller, less-formed tillers may die off at this stage.
Booting	You can see the head of the wheat forming beneath the sheath on the stalk.
Head and Flower Stage	All the plants in the field should flower at the same time.
Maturity	The kernels of grain form, grow and dry.

IDENTIFY THE GRAINS

Draw a line from each image to the correct grain type.

BARLEY

WHEAT

RYE

OATS

WORD SEARCH

```
R F O O D V A R I E T Y G Z C J R
E A X T Q F A E V O L U T I O N E
L M C R S B G K B A R L E Y Y C V
L Y H C R A R E I H L A I C O S O
I J N U T R I T I O N H Q S S F L
T U O E A G R I C U L T U R E E U
Y T P I Q B C M T Y Q L Q H P T T
Y P S V N Q G S Y T D A Y B R A I
E A D E M T E A R N M E W W J V O
X I C M V K I N F L O W E R P I N
T P V K A R N N I K J J I C O T R
K M K C Y N A X G L M P J M R L K
S E T A R D Y H O B R A C M R U A
N A V Y N O I T A Z I L I V I C O
O F I E L D S S M I L I Q N D I Z
D F G N I T O O B E Y E G P G N D
X Q F G G N I L D E E S M Q E U G
```

Agriculture	Cultivate	Harvest	Revolution
Barley	Evolution	Jointing	Seedling
Booting	Fields	Nutrition	Social Hierarchy
Carbohydrates	Flower	Oatcakes	Tiller
Civilization	Food Variety	Porridge	Wealth

INVENTION DISCUSSION PAGE

Name:_____ Date:_____

Invention/Product:_____

Who invented it?_____ When?_____

How does it work?
_____
_____
_____

What problem did it solve?
_____
_____
_____

What was it like before the product was invented? What did people use or do instead?
_____
_____
_____

Who could own it? (Did everyone get to use it? Was it expensive? Was it easy to get?)
_____
_____
_____

Can anyone use this product? What skill was needed to operate it?
_____
_____
_____

Is the product still in use today? How has it changed since its original invention?
_____
_____
_____

WHEEL

4,500 BCE

The wheel is often thought of as one of the first inventions, but it actually arrived near the transition from Stone Age to Bronze Age.

Evidence of wheels has been found from Europe to the Middle East to Asia but no one really knows who invented it. It could have been anyone across those continents, or perhaps several people did so at different times due to similar needs.

The potters' wheel was used around 6,500 years ago (about 4,500 BCE) in the Near East. Mesopotamians started mining and manipulating copper soon after and will have needed a way to haul the materials. Besides, the Agricultural Revolution created a demand for growing, harvesting, and delivering large quantities of grain. Thus, there was a new need for a way to transport heavy loads over land. Wheeled carts would have solved that need.

Perhaps someone watched a potter's wheel roll away and likened it to a log rolling. The first wheels for carts were made of wood, probably a slice of log, with a hole punched through the center for an axle. You can see evidence of wheeled carts and wagons on clay tablets from Eurasia and the Middle East, roughly 5,400 years old. People in this region had by then built large cities and huge structures, and they had become masters of agriculture.

Sources:

1. Bellis, Mary. "The Invention of the Wheel." ThoughtCo, Feb. 11, 2021, https://www.thoughtco.com/the-invention-of-the-wheel-1992669
2. Wikipedia. Wheel. Available at: https://en.wikipedia.org/wiki/Wheel. Accessed May 25, 2023.
3. Smithsonian Magazine. A Salute to the Wheel. Available at: https://www.smithsonianmag.com/science-nature/a-salute-to-the-wheel-31805121/. Accessed May 26, 2023.

READING, WRITING, RESEARCH

Level 1:

1. Learn about how the wheel and axle work using Legos. Visit https://education.lego.com/en-us/lessons/sm/wheels-and-axles#connect.

2. Did you know everyday objects like doorknobs, scissors, and toilet flushers use wheels to help them work? How many more items that use a wheel can you find in your home, classroom, or community?

3. Make up a story of the first person to invent the wheel. Start the story with a need that can be solved with a wheel. Then tell how someone gets the idea to make a wheel. Finish up with how the wheel made life better for the people.

Level 2:

1. Learn about the wheel and axle and other simple machines. Visit https://www.nationalgeographic.org/activity/simple-machine-challenge/ or https://www.livescience.com/49106-simple-machines.html. Explain what would happen if your wheel didn't have an axle. How would it fail? How can you make it work?

2. Without a wheel, explain how else ancient people might have transported heavy loads.

3. Research to learn who invented the wheelbarrow. Tell how historians know this.

Level 3:

1. Research and learn about "work," "stored energy," and "inertia." Explain how the wheel can fit into each of these processes.

2. Take a virtual tour to learn about Mesopotamia at: https://education.nationalgeographic.org/resource/ancient-mesopotamia-101/.

3. Write a report about when, how, and where the Mesopotamian Empire began; list its contributions to humanity; and explain how it changed over time until its downfall.

STEAM ACTIVITIES AND MORE

Level 1

1. Build a car or truck out of Legos. Explain how the wheel and axles work when you use them.

2. Draw a diagram of how a wheel uses an axle to make it work.

3. Make a pinwheel. Parents can search up a pattern to cut out. You'll need sturdy paper; a stick (pencil with eraser works well); a thumbtack or push pin; and a button or small piece of heavy cardboard to use as a washer (or spacer). You can decorate your pinwheel if you want!

Level 2

1. Place a brick on a flat surface. Push it across the surface with your hand. Was it easy or hard to do? Now line up several pencils [like this: ||||] on the table and lay the brick on top. Try to push the brick across the table. Which worked easier: with the pencils or without? Why do you think so?

2. Roll a single button, washer, or another wheel-type object down a ramp. What happens to it? Now attach two of the same objects to an axle and roll down the same ramp. How did the result change? What more can you do to make it even better?

3. Build a mousetrap-powered car. Search online for "How to build a mousetrap car" or go to https://www.wikihow.com/Build-a-Mousetrap-Car. Watch your fingers! As an alternative, you can build a balloon-powered car.

Level 3

1. Using your knowledge of simple machines, stored energy, and inertia, build a car using toilet paper tubes as the wheels. You can use any other objects to build your car, but the toilet paper tubes must serve as the wheels. Then have a race with someone else, or try to improve the speed of your own car.

2. "Invent" a small water wheel using everyday household items such as paper cups.

Coloring page

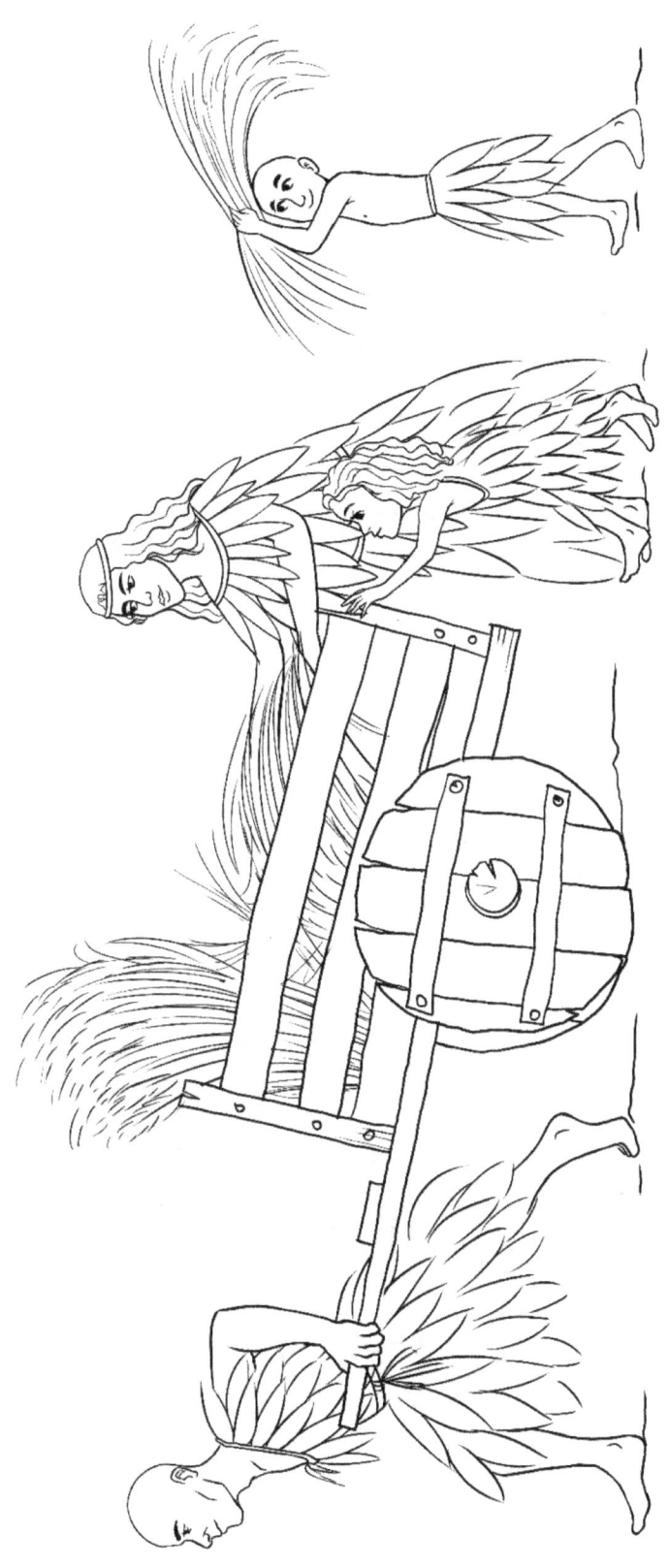

HISTORY UNSCHOOLED INVENTIONS FROM THE STONE AGE | 73

Wheel Maze

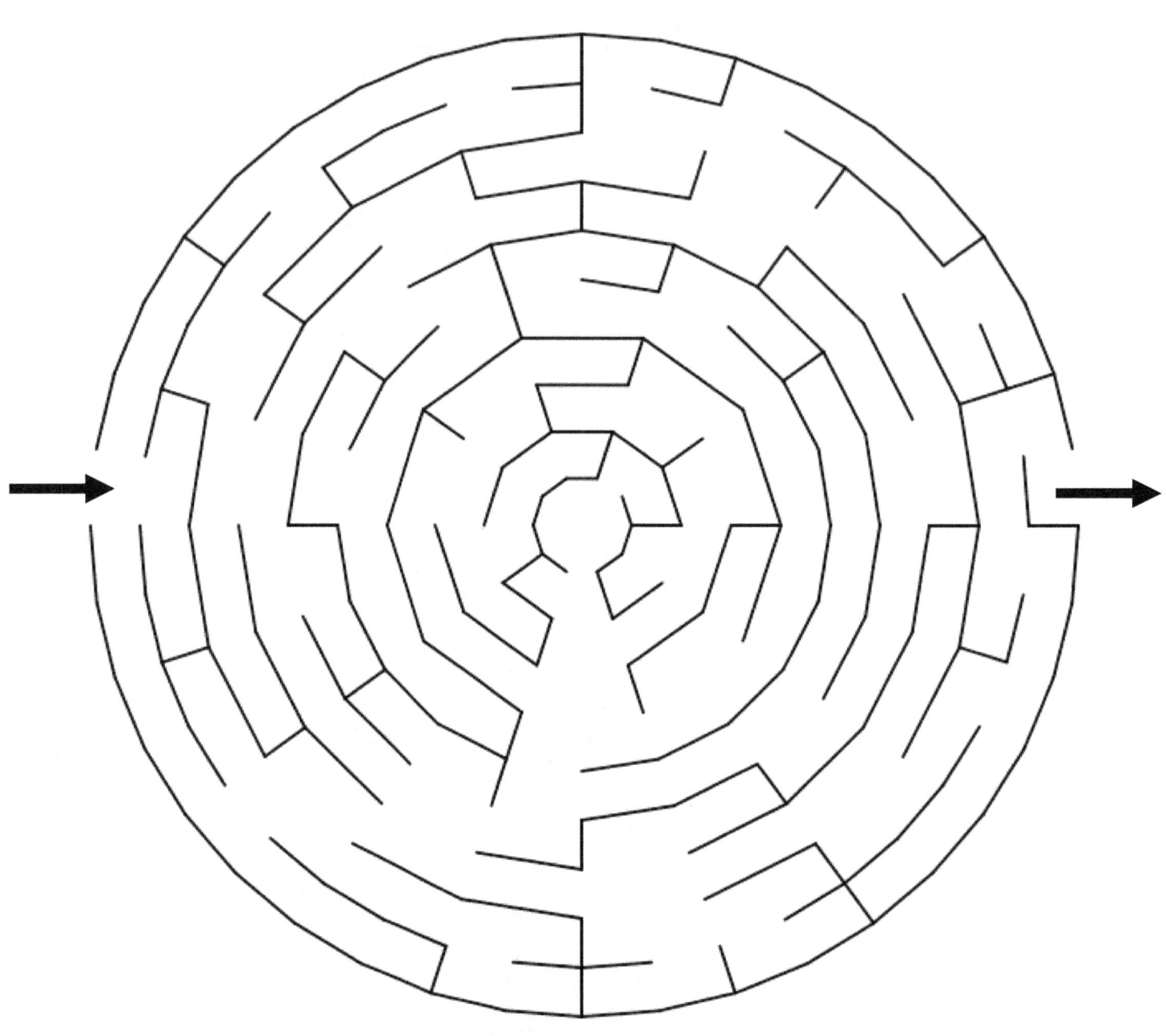

INVENTION DISCUSSION PAGE

Name:_____ Date:_____

Invention/Product:_____

Who invented it?_____ When?_____

How does it work?
_____
_____
_____

What problem did it solve?
_____
_____
_____

What was it like before the product was invented? What did people use or do instead?
_____
_____
_____

Who could own it? (Did everyone get to use it? Was it expensive? Was it easy to get?)
_____
_____
_____

Can anyone use this product? What skill was needed to operate it?
_____
_____
_____

Is the product still in use today? How has it changed since its original invention?
_____
_____
_____

PUZZLE SOLUTIONS

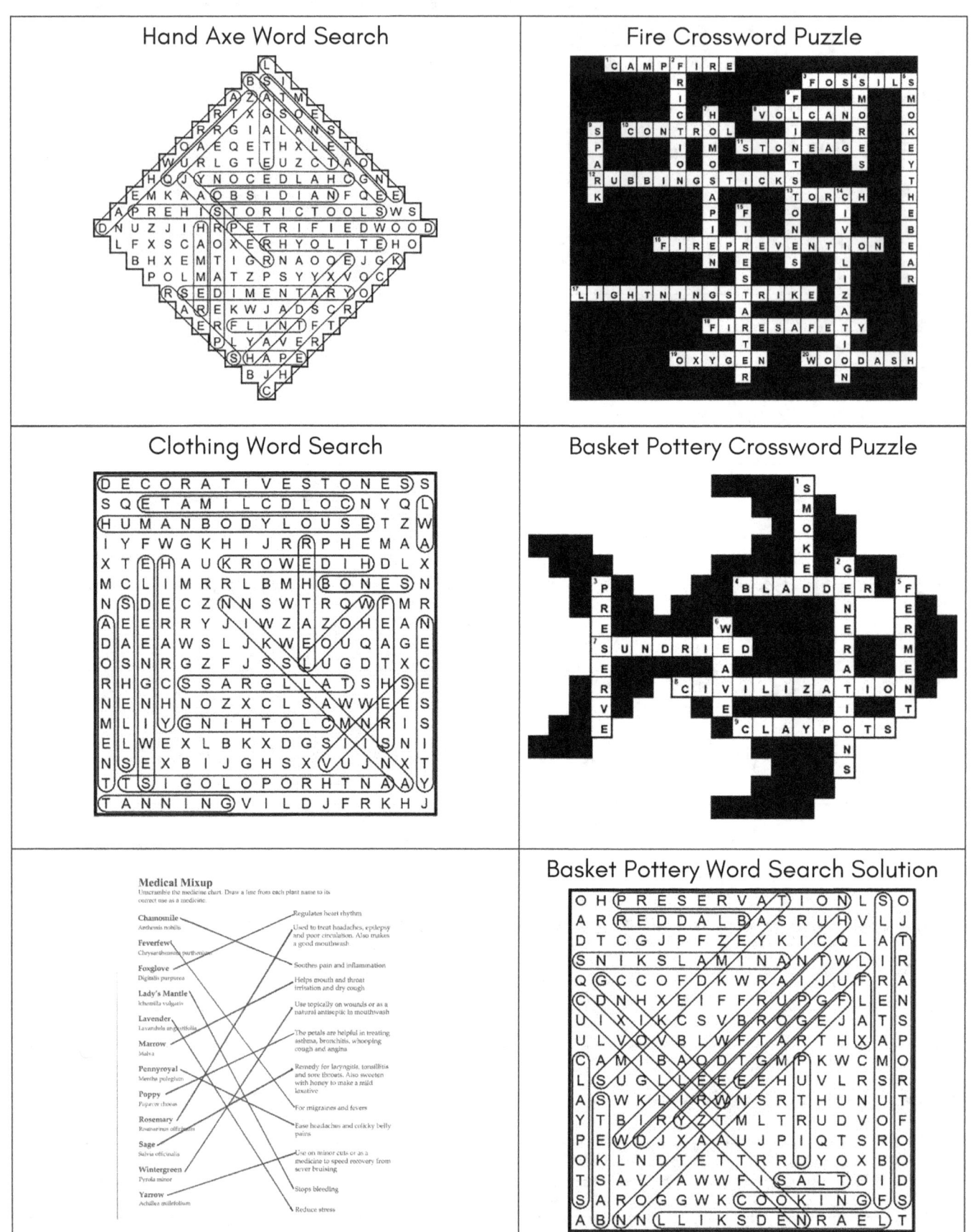

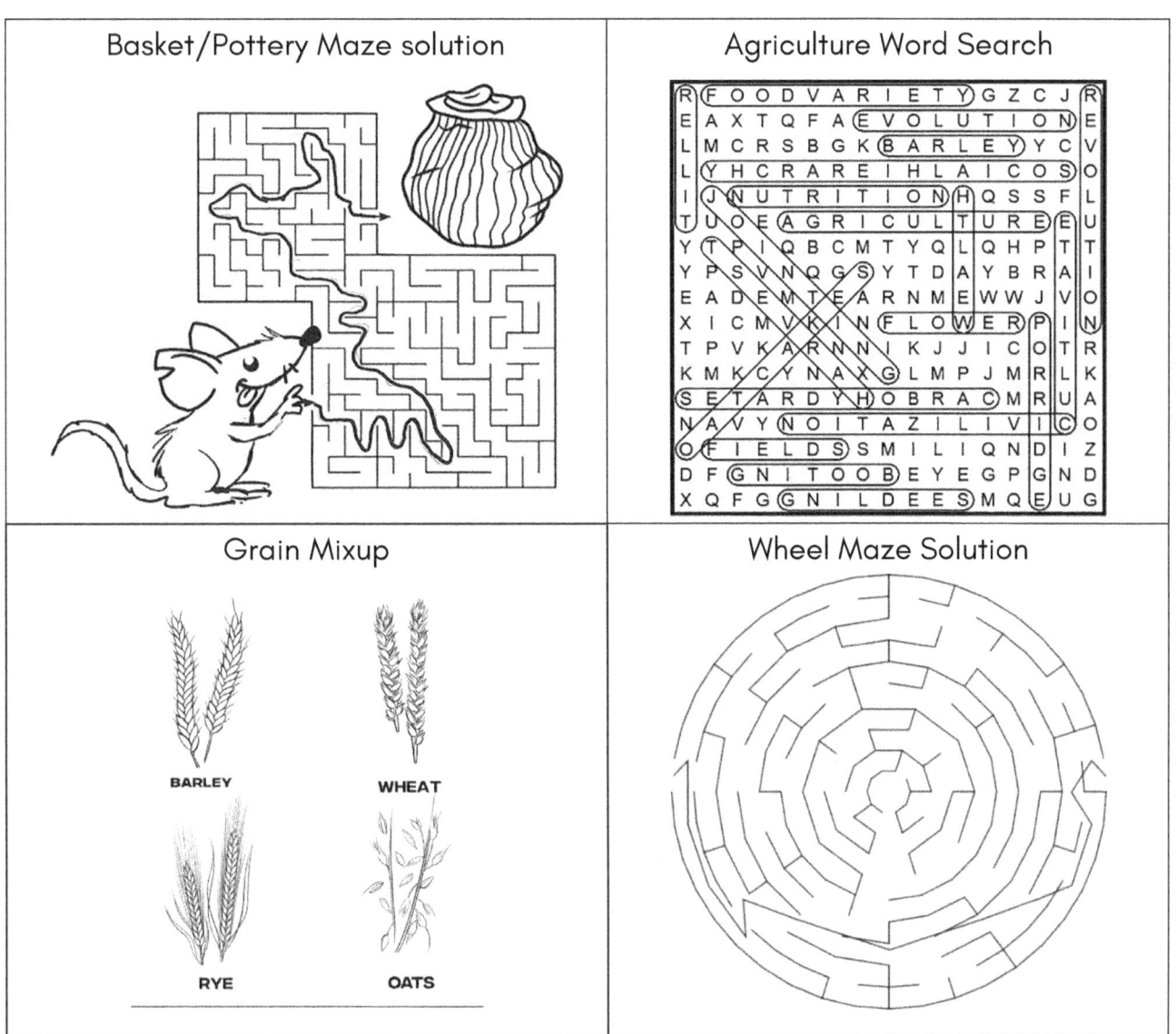

HISTORY UNSCHOOLED INVENTIONS FROM THE STONE AGE | 77

www.ingramcontent.com/pod-product-compliance
Lightning Source LLC
Chambersburg PA
CBHW081158070526
44583CB00021B/2893